THE HOUSE OF THE HEART
IS NEVER FULL
AND
OTHER PROVERBS OF AFRICA

GUY A. ZONA

A TOUCHSTONE BOOK
PUBLISHED BY SIMON & SCHUSTER
NEW YORK LONDON TORONTO SYDNEY TOKYO SINGAPORE

Touchstone

Rockefeller Center
1230 Avenue of the Americas
New York, New York 10020
Copyright © 1993 by Guy A. Zona
First Touchstone Edition 1993
Simon & Schuster, Touchstone, and colophon are registered trademarks
of Simon & Schuster Inc.
Designed by Irving Perkins Associates
Manufactured in the United States of America
3 5 7 9 10 8 6 4 2
Library of Congress Cataloging in Publication Data
Zona, Guy.
The house of the heart is never full and other proverbs of Africa
/ by Guy A. Zona.—1st Touchstone ed.
p.   cm.
"A Touchstone book."
1. Proverbs, African.   I. Title.
PN6519.A6Z66   1993
398.9′096—dc20   93-19907   CIP
ISBN 0-671-79731-X

INTRODUCTION

PROVERBS are age-old wisdom stated in a few words; sometimes they are our only links to the history and culture of a people otherwise unrecorded. European proverbs speak of oaks and horses, those of Asia speak of bamboo and buffalo, and those of Africa speak of palm trees and camels. However, their message is the same: differences exist between the peoples and races of the world, but our values, philosophies, and wisdom vary only in the setting from which they originate.

It is said that the truest picture of a people is to be found in their proverbs. These pithy, sometimes enigmatic sayings allow us to reach within a culture and extract the knowledge and beliefs handed down from one generation to the next. As the great river Nile is fed by smaller tributaries, the flow of African culture is fed by the extraordinary diversity of its people from primitive hunter/gatherers like the Pygmies of the Congo to the Ashantis of Ghana with their complex and sophisticated society.

In the following pages you will find proverbs both traditional and modern, reflecting Africa's many cultures and peoples. They speak of every aspect of life: community, family, marriage, deity, morality, ethics, charity, government, and law.

Read them, and learn.

Guy A. Zona

A needle can't hold two threads or a mind two thoughts.

❖

"Come and I'll tell you" tickles the ear.

❖

The camel never sees its own hump, but that of its brothers is always before its eyes.

❖

When we fell trees in the forest, we ought to imagine the situation reversed.

The word "yes" brings trouble; the word "no" leads to no evil.

⬥

When you invite a tortoise to a meal it is no use giving him water to wash his paws, because he will soon walk on the ground and dirty them.

⬥

Do not blame God for having created the tiger, but thank Him for not having given it wings.

⬥

Strife never begets a gentle child.

Clouds do not always denote rain, but smoke is always a sign of fire.

❖

A heavy burden does not kill on the day it is carried.

❖

The wrongdoer forgets, but not the wronged.

❖

Foolishness often precedes wisdom.

❖

Hurry bequeaths disappointment.

Distance suppresses the unpleasant.

◇

He who has only one garment doesn't wash it on a rainy day.

◇

Crooked wood makes crooked ashes.

◇

All is never said.

◇

The land is never void of counselors.

No sleep, no dream.

❖

Those whom we cannot catch we leave in the hands of God.

❖

The wisdom of this year is the folly of the next.

❖

When one gives bread to honorable men it is a loan, but to contemptible or dishonorable men it is charity.

The best remedy for a dispute is to discuss it.

❖

Wisdom has no dwelling of her own.

❖

Water is never tired of flowing.

❖

The priest will die; the doctor will depart this life; nor will the sorcerer be spared.

Privation has no voice and suffering cannot speak.

✧

To ask well is to know much.

✧

The parasite belongs to no class; it claims kinship with every tree.

✧

No matter how well an idol is made, it must have something to stand on.

What is really a load should not be called an ornament.

❖

He on whose head we would break a coconut never stands still.

❖

Ask for help and you will see those who never oblige; ask for alms and you will see the misers.

❖

There is a measure for corn in cases of dispute; in just the same way the world has a standard.

Reason has no age.

✧

Ears usually witness a matter without invitation.

✧

There are no cattle without a dung heap.

✧

That which brings misfortune is not big.

✧

It is the influence of the fountain which causes the stream to flow.

The key that opens is also the key that locks.

❖

If a bullet fired in malice does not draw blood where it starts, it will draw blood where it strikes.

❖

The man who is not hungry says the coconut has a hard shell.

❖

A hare is like an ass in the length of its ears, yet it is not its son.

There are forty kinds of lunacy, but only one kind of common sense.

✧

It is best to let an offense repeat itself at least three times: the first offense may be an accident, the second a mistake, but the third is likely to be intentional.

✧

Pride goes only as far as one can spit.

✧

The marvelous and the astonishing surprise only for a week.

The little stars always shine while the great sun is often eclipsed.

❖

The African race is a rubber ball; the harder you dash it to the ground, the higher it will rise.

❖

Gratitude is a lotus flower whose leaves soon wither.

❖

Wisdom is not a medicine to be swallowed.

Don't try to get blood from a locust; God didn't put it there.

✧

A load of salt on another man's head is easily carried.

✧

The stone in the water does not know that the hill in the sun is parched.

✧

What one hopes for is better than what one finds.

✧

It is not the eye that understands but the mind.

To look at the green adorns the heart and the eye.

✦

From contentment with little comes happiness.

✦

Everybody who is praised will be despised.

✦

The world has not given a promise to anybody.

✦

Every sheep hangs by its own leg.

Where are the cattle, there the wolf shall die.

❖

If you know the beginning well, the end will not trouble you.

❖

The tree that is not taller than you cannot shade you.

❖

Nothing can suffice a man except what he has not.

❖

Once the executioner has cut off the head he is not afraid of anything again.

Earth is the queen of beds.

✧

Were there no elephants in the jungle, the buffalo would be large.

✧

What lowers itself is ready to fall.

✧

A good case is not difficult to state.

✧

When the mouse laughs at the cat, there is a hole nearby.

If nothing touches the palm leaves they do not rustle.

✧

It is the dog's master who can take the bone from its mouth.

✧

If one could not make use of gold dust, it would merely be
called sand.

✧

One tree receiving all the wind breaks.

Take what the gods give while their hands are open, for none know what they will withhold when they are shut.

✧

The tyrant is only the slave turned inside out.

✧

If there were no fault, there would be no pardon.

✧

Even if the elephant is thin he is still the lord of the forest.

✧

The eyes believe themselves; the ears believe others.

The world is like a dancing girl; it dances to everyone for a little while.

✧

For the sake of the rose the thorn is watered.

✧

The words of the night are coated with butter; as soon as the sun shines they melt away.

✧

A man is safe when alone.

Even in time of drought one may still see dew.

❖

Hope is the pillar of the world.

❖

Everything that has a beginning has an end.

❖

Sorrow is like a cloud; when it becomes heavy it falls.

❖

Sorrow is like rice in the store; if a basketful is removed every day, it comes to an end at last.

Don't be like the shadow: a constant companion yet not a comrade.

◇

Water doesn't refuse to fall, or smoke to rise.

◇

Better a clever enemy than a blundering friend.

◇

The fuel in the lamp consumes itself but lights others.

◇

News does not sleep on the way.

Powder doesn't refuse fire, or fire fuel.

❖

The snake bites where he has reached.

❖

The stick that is to save you is found in your hand.

❖

The iron has no power over the smith.

❖

When the master is absent, the frogs climb into the house.

The stick in your neighbor's house is of no use against the leopard at your door.

✧

That which is deadly may have a sweet scent.

✧

Caution is not cowardice; even the ants march armed.

✧

Cunning does not kill the fish; the killer of the fish is the net.

✧

We do not know the child of wealth by his size.

"Let us go" doesn't mean a journey.

✧

The fire at which you don't warm yourself gives you no blisters.

✧

The cultivator is one; the eaters are many.

✧

An elephant's death throes are not so annoying as the life of a bug.

Today before tomorrow.

✧

If sweetness is excessive, it is no longer sweetness.

✧

Wits are wealth.

✧

Fire does not produce fire, it produces ashes.

✧

The fish in the trap begin to think.

A man follows that which floats; he does not follow that which sinks.

✧

There are three things that a man must know to survive long in the world: what is too much for him, what is too little for him, and what is just right for him.

✧

Nobody praises the living.

✧

The pot will smell of what is put into it.

He who recognizes the disease is the physician.

✧

A little bird for a little cage.

✧

Do not borrow from the world, for the world will require its own back with interest.

✧

A coconut shell full of water is a sea to an ant.

The miser is a thief.

✧

Greatness is not secured by violence.

✧

Sweet things never fill a spoon.

✧

A snake you see does not bite.

✧

Where there is a corpse, vultures assemble.

A reflection does not see itself.

◇

That which is made forgets—the maker forgets not.

◇

To bid farewell causes people to be strangers.

◇

The hollow of the ear is never full.

◇

The fruit that is not yet ripe doesn't fall to the ground.

That which is exceptionally good is a forerunner of something bad.

✧

Money softens a dispute as water softens clay.

✧

Numerous calls confuse the dog.

✧

The child whom you send to the capital to salute the king pays court on his own account.

Why criticize what you have not cooked?

✧

What was used to make the world will also be used to destroy it.

✧

The hippopotamus that shows itself doesn't upset the boat.

✧

One small straw suffices to remove the honey from the hive.

Hit one ring and the whole chain will resound.

✧

Cleverness eats its owner.

✧

Even a large ship may be wrecked in darkness.

✧

A river is filled by its tributaries.

✧

Only what you have eaten is yours; other things may not be.

Swiftness has an end, but the racecourse remains.

✧

The poultry yard will be built up when the hyena has killed the fowls.

✧

Small matters breed important ones.

✧

Guilt never decays.

It doesn't dawn only on one day; tomorrow the sun will shine also.

❖

The breaking day has wisdom, the falling day experience.

❖

Live patiently in the world; know that those who hate you are more numerous than those who love you.

❖

There are three friends in this world: courage, sense, and insight.

A frown is not a slap.

◇

If you see a goat at the lion's sleeping place, you fear her.

◇

Doing mischief is more pleasant than repairing it.

◇

Disregard its small size; the needle is steel.

◇

A man does not run among thorns for no reason; either he is chasing a snake or a snake is chasing him.

Hunt in every jungle, for there is wisdom and good hunting in all of them.

✧

Food you will not eat you do not boil.

✧

One man is another man's obstacle.

✧

If a great man should wrong you, smile on him.

One sits on a crooked tree to fell a straight one.

✧

Cross the river before you insult the crocodile.

✧

Taking thought is strength.

✧

What is in the stomach carries what is on the head.

✧

The bird that goes on living always gets new feathers.

It is the expert swimmer whom the river carries away.

✧

The rain does not recognize anyone as a friend; it drenches whomever it sees.

✧

One day of rain far surpasses a whole year of drought.

✧

He who drives an ass must of necessity smell its wind.

The camel-driver has his plans and the camel has his.

✧

The very fact that we are seeking a thing usually stands in the way of our finding it.

✧

An old story does not open the ear as a new one does.

✧

He who knows us is not like him we know.

✧

''Nearly'' is an individual we invariably meet on the way.

He ought to be feared who sends you with a message, not he to whom you are sent.

❖

If you would make a dog come to you, don't hold a stick in your hand.

❖

The child of the savior is not saved.

❖

When the ape cannot reach the ripe banana with his hand, he says it is sour.

Travel and you will see them, sit and they will come to you.

✧

Never follow a beast into its lair.

✧

A drop of water on a field is riches; a drop of water on a viper is poison.

✧

Do not show caterpillars leaves.

Give to the earth and the earth will give to you.

◈

To take revenge is often to sacrifice oneself.

◈

Thirst cannot be quenched by proxy.

◈

A knife does not know its master.

◈

Though a leopard give birth to a palm rat, she does not eat it.

An egg in the mouth is better than a hen in the coop.

❖

Say "no" from the first; you will have rest.

❖

He who seeks a thing will find it, and he who hides a thing
will lose it.

❖

If you see ants on the staircase, know that there is semolina
upstairs.

Going slowly doesn't prevent one from arriving.

✧

The hand that you cannot bite, kiss.

✧

Follow the holy man no farther than his threshold.

✧

Don't say you have beans until they are in the measure.

✧

Clouds are not hurt by the barking of dogs.

Cupidity is a plague, and plague kills.

✧

Slowness comes from God and quickness from the devil.

✧

He who does not know is forgiven by God.

✧

Haste is the sister of repentance.

✧

Ask of him who has been satisfied and is now hungry; don't ask of him who has been hungry and is now satisfied.

Leave the thing that leaves you.

❖

Be a lion and eat me; don't be a dog and worry me.

❖

He who betrays one that betrays him not, Allah shall betray him.

❖

If a man makes soup of his tears, do not ask him for broth.

It is while one still has the old bucket that one should make a new one.

✧

Fear the noble if you make little of him; fear the base man if you honor him.

✧

Noise and hunting don't go together.

✧

Nothing wipes your tears away but your own hand.

If you owe a dog anything, call him "sir."

⋄

If the moon is with you, you need not care about the stars.

⋄

If nothing has ever done you any harm, you will never have foresight.

⋄

Eating little drives away many complaints.

Even if the tree snake is long, he can't sleep on two anthills at once.

✧

When the meat is done, you come to the chopping board.

✧

Don't help a bull out of a ditch, for when he's out he'll butt you.

✧

He who takes a light to find the whereabouts of a snake should start at his own feet.

What does not kill the herdsman will not touch his cows.

❖

Who makes you pay in tears, you make him pay in blood.

❖

If you wait until the whole animal appears, you will only spear the tail.

❖

The stick which you have by you is the one with which you will kill the snake.

Unless you stop the crack you will rebuild a wall.

❖

Don't ask me where I am going but where I have come from.

❖

He who waits for the moon waits for darkness.

❖

He who has not carried your burden does not know what it weighs.

❖

Medicine that is mixed with food, even if it doesn't cure the disease, will cure hunger.

Always being in a hurry does not prevent death, neither does going slowly prevent living.

❖

Delay does not spoil things; it makes them better.

❖

When an elephant chases you, you climb a prickly tree.

❖

One will never lack a mane if one looks in the stable.

❖

I do not sow ground nuts when the monkey is watching.

Practice with the left hand while the right is still there.

✧

The rain does not always fall when it threatens.

✧

One good thing leaves another; milk leaves butter.

✧

When you have no stick, the mouse passes close to you.

✧

If you want to tell anything to God, tell it to the wind.

For the sake of the book the binding is loved.

❖

Be patient of little; God will give you much.

❖

He who gives to God does not go to bed hungry.

❖

When a man doesn't call, God does.

❖

What God has sent does not fail to reach the earth.

In hell there are no fans.

❖

If God should count our sins, we should perish.

❖

Repose in God and sleep with a snake.

❖

Manage with bread and butter until God brings the jam.

❖

To commit ten sins against God is better than to commit one against a servant of God.

To every field of wheat God sends its reaper.

❖

Give it for the sake of God and give it even to him who does not believe in God.

❖

The plant God favors will grow even without rain.

❖

God portions out blessings; if a man distributed them, some would go without.

Every knot has an unraveler in God.

✧

God made the sea, we make the ship; He made the wind, we make a sail; He made the calm, we make oars

✧

God does not forget the ant in its little hole.

✧

One may go around a ravine or around a hill but one cannot go around God.

God gives and does not remind us continually of it; the world gives and constantly reminds us.

✧

Hell itself holds dishonor in horror.

✧

In doing good, one does it to oneself; in doing evil, one does it to all.

✧

It is better to spend the night in irritation at an offense than in repentance for taking revenge.

Conceal the good you do; take example from the Nile, which hides its source.

✧

The world is a mirror: show yourself in it and it will reflect your image.

✧

Learn politeness from the impolite.

✧

The bitter heart eats its owner.

Truth and the morning become light with time.

❖

A promise is a debt.

❖

On the palm tree of glory the date of modesty withers.

❖

A lie can give more pain than a spear.

❖

You who condemn on hearsay evidence alone, your sins increase.

Evil is a hill; everyone gets up on his own and proclaims that of another.

✧

Do good; you will find good.

✧

Soap cleans a garment, and mercy cleans the heart.

✧

The medicine for hate is separation.

✧

Forgiveness from the heart is better than a box of gold.

If you have much, give from your wealth; and if you have little, give from your heart.

✦

Kindness can pluck a lion's whiskers.

✦

Cruelty is the strength of the wicked.

✦

Greed loses what it has gained.

✦

A man's deeds are his life.

One achieves more with patience than with anger.

❖

It is the heart that carries one to hell or heaven.

❖

Thanks are due to the shoulders that keep the shirt from slipping off.

❖

Hate has no medicine.

❖

Inordinate gain makes a hole in the pocket.

He that forgives gains the victory.

✧

If we hurl a stone into a market, it is usually our own kith and kin whom it hits in the eye.

✧

Beautify your tongue; you will obtain what you desire.

✧

Don't do good by halves.

Guilt repented of becomes righteousness, but righteousness boasted of becomes the grandfather of guilt.

◇

The end of an ox is beef and the end of a lie is exposure.

◇

Scandal is like an egg; when it is hatched it has wings.

◇

The judgment of the world comes to us every day.

◇

If your intention is pure, you can walk on the sea.

Do well today on account of tomorrow.

❖

The body prostrated on the ground does not make humility.

❖

Truth keeps the hands cleaner than soap.

❖

If a grain of corn falls in the mud, the inside is still white.

❖

Respect depends on reciprocity.

Not to aid one in distress is to kill him in your heart.

✧

He who has wheat should lend flour.

✧

Hand and tongue never give alike.

✧

Whoever loves you, even a dog, you will also love.

✧

The way to the beloved is not thorny.

The house of the heart is never full.

✧

When the heart undertakes, the body is its slave.

✧

Love is like seaweed; even if you have pushed it away, that will not prevent its coming back.

✧

Sore eyes are seen, but a sore heart is hidden.

Mutual love is often better than natural brotherhood.

✧

The greatness of love obliterates conventions.

✧

Marriage takes a night; the thinking of it a year.

✧

Love me as you do cotton; add to the thin and rejoin the broken.

Let your love be like misty rain; gentle in coming but flooding the river.

✧

Where the heart desires, there it goes.

✧

The disease of love has no physician.

✧

That of which one's heart is full slips onto the tongue.

✧

He who loves the vase loves also what is inside.

It is better for the eyes to die than the heart.

✧

If one finger is gashed, all the fingers are covered with blood.

✧

If you know his father and grandfather, don't worry about his son.

✧

Brethren love each other when they are equally rich.

Brotherly love is like thread in the needle, unless it projects beyond the eye, it will not profit.

❖

He is a near relative while there are shrimps to be had, but when they are done, he is only a distant relative.

❖

The ties established between two families by a happy marriage are stronger than those of money.

❖

The horse never refuses a homeward gallop.

It is the place one lives in that one repairs.

✧

Every beast roars in its own den.

✧

A small house will hold a hundred friends.

✧

To where the heart has rejoiced at night, one returns in the morning.

✧

You need not tell a child that there is a God.

It is not difficult to fill a child's hand.

❖

The child hates him who gives it all it wants.

❖

If you love the children of others, you will love your own even better.

❖

Instruction in youth is like engraving in stones.

❖

The best protection against death is giving birth.

The gazelle jumps, and should her child crawl?

❖

Children talk with God.

❖

He who has children has blessings.

❖

The calves do not fear the horns of their mother.

❖

It is the path of the needle that the thread is accustomed to follow.

Fingers are not of equal length.

❖

Don't let charity go out of your house until the children are satisfied.

❖

A child who asks questions isn't stupid.

❖

Wealth of children comes first, money second.

He who is not chastised by his parents is chastised by his ill wisher.

✧

That child is loved most who is young until he is grown up, or sick until he recovers, or absent until he returns home.

✧

If you refuse to be made straight when you are green, you will not be made straight when you are dry.

✧

The son of a snake is a snake.

A father can feed seven children, but seven children can't feed one father.

◇

The chicks of man take long to fly.

◇

The egg teaches the hen how to hatch.

◇

Quick loving a woman means quick not loving a woman.

◇

Two crocodiles don't live in one pond.

If men swear to do you harm, spend your night sleeping, but if women swear to do you harm, spend your night awake.

✧

A woman's strength is a multitude of words.

✧

Men and women toward each other are for the eyes and for the heart, and not only for the bed.

✧

Paradise is open at the command of mothers.

He who is not taught by his mother will be taught by the world.

✧

Marriage is not tied with a fast knot but with a slipknot.

✧

Strife sleeps in the house of the man with two wives.

✧

Seven children won't hold a husband but plenty of wisdom will.

What happens to your wife happens to yourself.

◆

A man's folly is not made so public as a woman's.

◆

Hold a true friend with both your hands.

◆

To be friends with a wild beast is better than to be friends with an inquisitive person.

Settle accounts with me as if I were your enemy and entertain me as your brother.

❖

A descent for the sake of a friend is an ascent.

❖

A stone from the hand of a friend is an apple.

❖

A powerful friend becomes a powerful enemy.

Without human companions, paradise itself would be an undesirable place.

❖

Through others I am somebody.

❖

A man's friends are as many as his enemies.

❖

Though a man has actually less wisdom than his friend, the friend treats him as though he had more.

Friendship that is kept up only while eyes see eyes does not go to the heart.

✧

The more intimate the friendship the deadlier the enmity.

✧

Be brothers, but keep accounts.

✧

Receiving honor won't make you a noble, and giving honor won't make you a slave, so it is well to honor one another.

Don't make it a dog's friendship, to be broken over a bone.

✦

He who betrays you is not one from afar.

✦

The man who escorts you through the night wins your gratitude at daybreak.

✦

Friendship is like a tailor's seam; it is the undoing that causes trouble.

Even a little thing brings friendship to remembrance.

❖

Words are easy, friendship hard.

❖

The wound given by a friend does not heal.

❖

He who doesn't say it to you isn't your friend.

❖

If you go to the sparrows' ball, take ears of corn for them.

Choose the neighbor before the house and the companion before the road.

✦

Your neighbor who is near is better than your brother who is far away.

✦

He who eats the fowls of others should fatten his own.

✦

Treat your elder as your father, your junior as your son, and your equal as your brother.

Not where I was born but where it goes well with me is my home.

❖

A good deed will make a good neighbor.

❖

Sticks in a bundle are unbreakable.

❖

The quarrel of the sheep doesn't concern the goats.

❖

Unity among the cattle makes the lion lie down hungry.

When a tree falls it leans on its neighbor.

✧

Even though you may enter the house, you don't always enter the hearts.

✧

In battle, the saber does not know the head of the blacksmith who made it.

✧

What the tale-bearer gains is curses.

The news has been heard all around, but the party it most concerns is deaf.

✧

He will see his nose who lowers his eyes.

✧

The morning of one's life foreshadows the eve.

✧

The thrower of stones flings away the strength of his own arm.

When you are warned, warn yourself.

✧

Every ambitious man is a captive and every covetous one a pauper.

✧

One who does what he says is not a coward.

✧

He whose mother is naked is not likely to clothe his aunt.

He who has been stung by a serpent fears a rope on the ground.

❖

He who makes a knot knows how to loose it.

❖

Not until we have fallen do we know how to rearrange our burden.

❖

Ashes always fly back in the face of him who throws them.

He who chatters to you will chatter of you.

✧

He who treats you as himself does you no injustice.

✧

Do not laugh at the fallen; there may be slippery places ahead.

✧

If a man puts a rope around his neck, God will provide someone to pull it.

If I am to be prince, and you are to be prince, who is to drive the donkey?

✧

There are men who are keys to good and locks to evil.

✧

He who is carried does not realize that the town is far off.

✧

Where there is character, ugliness is beauty; where no character, beauty is ugliness.

Those who do not honor the law praise those who break it.

✧

Know how to meet and know how to part.

✧

There are people who will help you get your basket on your head because they want to see what's in it.

✧

A man is in his words.

Know yourself better than he does who speaks of you.

✧

The true believer begins with himself.

✧

Don't belittle him who is not small; don't magnify him who is not great.

✧

He who is dressed in other people's belongings is naked and he who is made satisfied by other people's belongings is hungry.

When cows are about to go out, they lick one another; when men are about to die, they love one another.

✧

It is on the path you do not fear that the wild beast catches you.

✧

The one-eyed man doesn't thank God until he sees a blind man.

✧

Keeping one's head exceeds in importance keeping one's hat.

He who learns to steal must learn to run.

✧

He who forgets the aim of his journey is still on the road.

✧

To trouble me is better than to forget me.

✧

The unfortunate man doesn't suffer from only one thing.

✧

Having choked, you are able to chew; having fallen, you are able to walk.

If you know what hurts yourself, you know what hurts others.

✧

Men don't all go one road.

✧

If you suffer in order to be beautiful, don't blame anyone but yourself.

✧

Leave a good name behind in case you return.

✧

He that pleases you not, do you please him?

If a man can live up to the reputation of a dog, he is a saint.

✧

He who endures ill is not taught.

✧

A man scratches where he can reach.

✧

People do not count what they are given but what is withheld from them.

✧

A man who is always crying is not listened to.

Don't show a hyena how well you can bite.

◇

The mouth is the heart's shield.

◇

A traveler with a tongue does not lose his way.

◇

No one can leave his character behind him when he goes on a journey.

The wise traveler leaves his heart at home.

✧

To rest on the road does not end the journey.

✧

While you are preparing to go on a journey, you own the journey, but after you have started, the journey owns you.

✧

Choose the road of safety even if it winds.

A long road brings out faults.

❖

He who does not travel will not know the value of men.

❖

The broken pitcher doesn't go to the waterhole.

❖

Good health is the recipe for wealth.

❖

Silence is also speech.

If I listen, I have the advantage; if I speak, they have it.

❖

Silence produces peace and peace produces safety.

❖

He who falls by his foot shall rise again; he who falls by his mouth shall not rise.

❖

The heart of a fool is in his mouth and the mouth of the wise man is in his heart.

▼▼

A chattering bird builds no nest.

✧

The greatest war is the war of the mouth.

✧

He who fills his head with other people's words will find no placc where he may put his own.

✧

The wound caused by words is worse than the wound of bodies.

They catch an ox by its horns, a man by his words.

◇

Hurry with your legs, not with your tongue.

◇

A cruel word is a wound of the heart; it does not heal, and even if it heals, the scar never departs.

◇

All they say will return to themselves.

◇

Rebuke the wise man and he will like you.

The supposition of the wise man is better than the certainty of the ignorant.

❖

Clever men do not bargain with one another.

❖

You have no wisdom if you go to sleep before you make your bed.

❖

The fool who owns an ox is seldom recognized as a fool.

❖

There is medicine for madness but none for foolishness.

The property of the grandfathers will come to an end, but the craft of the hands will remain.

✧

One drop after another fills the pot.

✧

Work is good provided you do not forget to live.

✧

The smaller the lizard the greater the hope of becoming a crocodile.

Compete, don't envy.

❖

Mend your clothes in a day; you will dress in them for a month.

❖

Doing one's best drives away regret.

❖

It is no good asking the spirits to help you run if you don't mean to sprint.

Dawn does not come twice to awaken a person.

✧

One doesn't forbid water to him who has dug the well.

✧

The drop of water one has drawn oneself tastes sweet.

✧

If spending your money gives you pain, you will go hungry.

✧

A good thing sells itself; a bad thing wants advertising.

A book is like a garden carried in the pocket.

✧

No one is without knowledge except him who asks no questions.

✧

The sight of books removes sorrows from the heart.

✧

He who knocks at the door will not go without an answer.

Wealth, if you use it, comes to an end; learning, if you use it, increases.

✧

You have your own salt; if it pleases you, you may use it to fry flies.

✧

With shoes on one can walk on thorns.

✧

The habitation of danger is on the borders of security.

Those who wear pearls do not know how often the shark bites the leg of the diver.

✧

Where there is more than enough, more than enough is wasted.

✧

He who has eaten doesn't make a fire for the hungry.

◊

Throw the fortunate man into the Nile and he will come out with a fish in his mouth.

There is no one who, being clad in one garment, will refuse a second.

People think that the poor are not so wise as the rich, for if a man be wise, why is he poor?

✧

The lack of powder converts a gun into a stick.

✧

Poverty without debt is real wealth.

✧

Where there is no wealth there is no poverty.

When a poor man makes a proverb it does not spread abroad.

❖

He who has the necessities has no shame.

❖

Hunger brings the crocodile out of the water.

❖

A man on the ground cannot fall.

❖

If the monkey reigns, prostrate thyself before him.

In a court of fowls, the cockroach never wins his case.

✧

One night of anarchy does more harm than a hundred years of tyranny.

✧

An unjust government is better than corrupt subjects.

✧

Beat the dog; the other dogs will run away.

✧

Force will never be without a place to sit down.

▼▼▼

Fright is worse than a blow.

✧

When your guns are few, your words are few.

✧

When elephants battle, the ants perish.

✧

It is better to thresh the corn than to sharpen the spear.

✧

Death does not recognize strength.

There is no medicine against old age.

❖

The dead are the best of his family.

❖

Along the road on which you are to meet your death, your legs will carry you and you will go.

❖

If we go forward we die; if we go backward we die; better go forward and die.

The tree that has been too much for the baboon the monkey cannot climb.

✧

When lizards eat pepper, it is the frog that perspires.

✧

A trap catches, even when covered with spider's webs.

✧

Brotherhood is neither bought nor sold.

Every matter of importance that is begun without the mention of God is maimed.

✧

There is nothing bigger than a rock, but as it doesn't speak, it is trodden on and soiled by the birds.

✧

If God opposes the destruction of an ant, He gives her wings.

✧

Lies buzz like flies, but truth has the brilliance of the sun.

▼▼▼

Let matrimony be like a fowl's clothing, not parted with until death.

✧

The viper takes the color of the country it lives in.

✧

A dog returns to where he has been fed.

✧

The bird that calls the rain will get wet itself.

▼▼▼

An elephant does not die of one broken rib.

✧

The snail leaves its slime wherever it goes.

✧